A Guide to Primitive Camping

Tips for Any Type of Outdoor Camping

JERRY DARSEY

Copyright © 2024 Jerry Darsey
All rights reserved
First Edition

NEWMAN SPRINGS PUBLISHING
320 Broad Street
Red Bank, NJ 07701

First originally published by Newman Springs Publishing 2024

ISBN 979-8-89061-353-0 (Paperback)
ISBN 979-8-89061-354-7 (Digital)

Printed in the United States of America

To the many fellow Boy Scouts, I went camping with.

CONTENTS

Preface ix

Chapter 1: Building a Shelter 1
Chapter 2: Building a Fire 9
Chapter 3: Finding and Purifying Water 12
Chapter 4: Obtaining Food 15
Chapter 5: Review of Significant Tips 22

Additional Reading 27
Index 31

FIGURE LEGENDS

Figure 1a–d: Showing the building of a lean-to shelter 3
Figure 2a–e: Steps for building a teepee shelter 6
Figure 3b–d: Steps for building a teepee fire structure 10
Figure 4: Showing using a bamboo stock for holding and
  boiling water 14
Figure 5: Showing walking stick with a forked end for
  catching snakes..16
Figure 6: Showing cavity fish trap made from vegetation 17
Figure 7: Showing funnel-shape tube trap for catching fish 18
Figure 8: Showing bucket trap with a ramp for catching
  small animals/crabs/crawfish...19
Figure 9: Showing setup of a snare trap 20

PREFACE

"It was the best of times, it was the worst of times."[1] These words were written by the great author Charles Dickens. They could easily describe many, if not most, campouts. Those who go camping on a regular or even an infrequent basis can relate to both "the best of times" and "the worst of times." If one is on a camping trip where the weather is good, the temperature is mild, there are few, if any, biting insects, and you're camping on a lake, river, or ocean, you would consider this camping trip "the best of times." However, if you go camping where the temperature is hot and steamy, the insects are eating you alive, and it starts raining, you probably would consider this camping trip "the worst of times." I have personally experienced both of these situations.

This book is primarily inspired by the TV show, *Naked and Afraid*. There were many instances where the participants did not seem to know many survival techniques. I have never appeared on this program, but I have been on many campouts, including survival campouts, while in the Explorer Boy Scouts. These campouts were mostly in the swamps of Louisiana. In Louisiana, we experienced many of the conditions seen on *Naked and Afraid*. I must confess that I have never tried to survive naked. I don't see any situation where one would find themselves without any clothing in a survival situation. I don't think even cavemen and cavewomen would need to survive naked. Therefore, I will not address any situation where one would find themselves naked since I find this situation highly improbable.

---

[1] Dickens, Charles, *A Tale of Two Cities*. Chapman & Hall, 1859

The primary audience of this book is those who would go on a primitive campout. However, many of the camping tips discussed in this book can be useful for any type of camping, from the one- to two-night camping trip to the enthusiast going on a one, two, or multiple-week primitive camping experience.

This book is divided into five chapters—chapter 1 deals with building a good survival shelter. Protecting yourself against the elements is very important. There's nothing worse than getting soaking wet and not being able to take cover from the rain. This potentially could become a very hazardous situation in which you get wet, and the temperature begins to fall. It doesn't take much for hyperthermia to set in. Chapter 2 discusses how to build a fire, which is one of the most important campout skills one can have. Chapter 3 is about securing a safe supply of water. In South Louisiana, finding water is not a problem. However, finding a safe, drinkable water supply is essential. You would never want to drink water straight from a bayou or a lake without purifying it. That requires boiling the water. If you have a pot, that shouldn't be a problem so long as you are successful at building a fire. If you do not have a pot, there will be tips in chapter 3 on how you can still boil water. Chapter 4 covers in detail how to secure food. There are many types of traps that one can learn to make in order to capture small animals. There are also techniques that can be used to catch fish without a hook. Chapter 5 will be a summary of all the tips that are discussed within the book. In addition, references will be provided for greater detail concerning some of the topics discussed in this book.

The last thing I want to mention, but the first thing you should do, is to find a good, strong walking stick. This walking stick should be about five to six feet in length and about one inch in circumference. Walking sticks will greatly facilitate walking; they can serve as a third leg. It helps in maintaining your balance, especially in rough terrain. It really helps when climbing or descending a steep incline. It can also act as a first line of defense against dangerous wildlife, including the possibility of snakes, bobcats, coyotes, wolves, and in the swamps of Louisiana, alligators.

CHAPTER 1

Building a Shelter

The first two most important tasks for someone in a primitive camping situation are to find water and make a shelter. In finding a suitable shelter location, many times, it will also point to a place where you can find water. (We will discuss the best ways to find water in chapter 3.) Of course, the environment you find yourself in determines what priority you give to either finding water or building a shelter first. If, in your situation, it is getting late, you may want to build your shelter first. For example, let's look at a situation where it is about two hours before sunset. If you are in an environment where it may get chilly and/or it may rain during the night, a shelter of some sort is very important! My recommendation is to make a "lean-to" shelter. These can be constructed fairly quickly and will provide at least some shelter from the elements. The next day, when you have more time, you might want to consider building a "teepee" type shelter.

Lean-to Shelter

Let's consider first a lean-to shelter. Start by collecting as wide a leaf material as possible. Look for palmetto leaves, palm tree leaves, banana tree leaves, or any other broad-leaf plant. You need a large stick or a branch that you could attach as a crossbar between two trees that are separated between four and six feet. You need to find vines or roots of vines as cordage (binding material). You need to place one crossbar branch between the two trees about four to five feet from the ground and bind it to the trees with your vine material (see figure 1). The direction in which you face your shelter needs to be taken into account. Try to face your shelter in a direction opposite of the possible wind or rain direction. Most of the time, you need to face your shelter south or east. That is because most rain fronts come from the north or northwest. This isn't always the case, but it is a good general rule. If you are close to a large body of water, you should point your shelter away from the water. It would also be wise not to build too close to any water source. There is always the possibility that a river or stream may overflow its banks during a heavy rainstorm. You should also consider the high tide when building near a large lake or the ocean. Another consideration should be to put one or more trees between your shelter and the water. Try to make sure the trees are stable with deep roots. You don't want the tree falling on your shelter in a strong wind. A third type of shelter you could build is an A-frame shelter, which is simply two lean-to shelters put together. See the bibliography for examples.

A GUIDE TO PRIMITIVE CAMPING

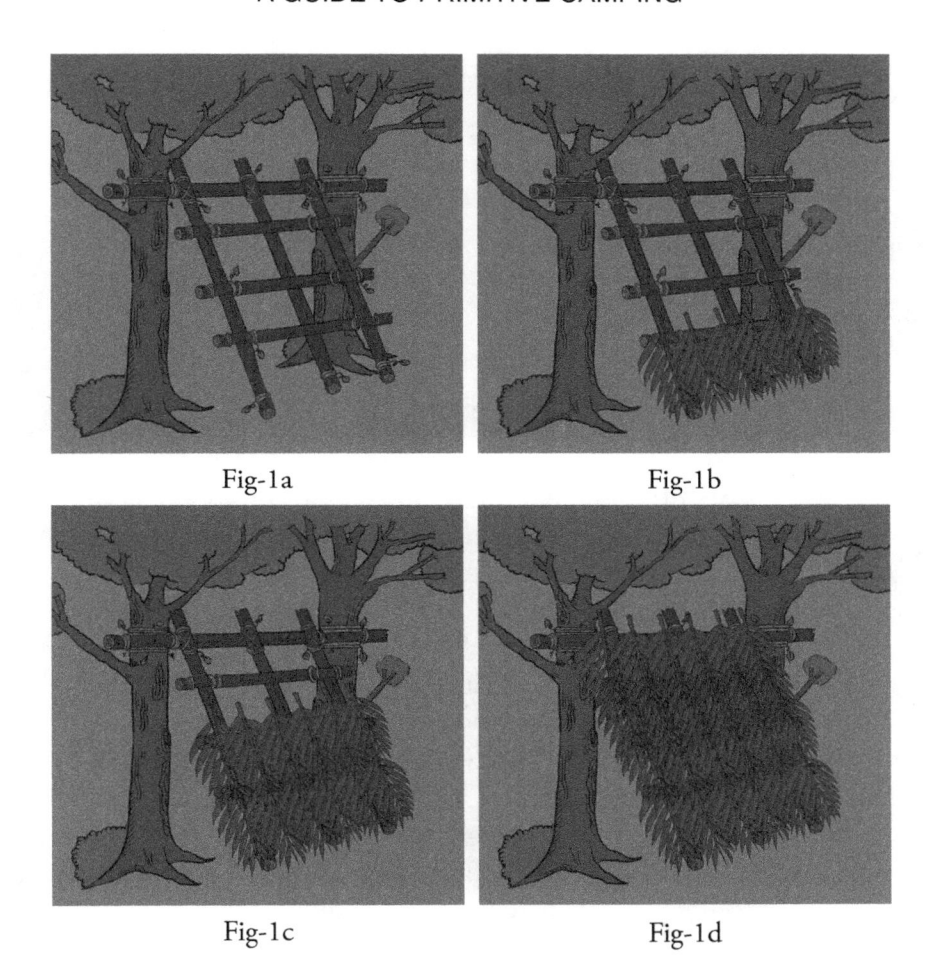

Fig-1a

Fig-1b

Fig-1c

Fig-1d

Figure 1a–d: Showing the building of a lean-to shelter

Now you need to have two long branches which will extend vertically from the crossbar branch to the ground (see fig. 1). Now place three or four more branches horizontally between the vertical branches, binding them with the vine material. These branches will support the leaves you will use to provide protection from the elements. You need to have the leaves pointed down toward the ground, and you need to lay the leaves starting from the bottom and going to the top. Securely attach each leaf with the vine material so they don't slide down or blow away in a strong wind. The final step in construction is to make a covering for the shelter floor. In Louisiana, we often used dead pine needles, which make excellent insulating material. If pine needles are not available, you can use any large leaf material, such as the leaves used to make the roof. You need to be sure you don't lie directly on the ground, which will cause a loss of much body heat. Make sure you check for insects in or on the leaves you use for ground cover.

Teepee Shelter

If time permits, on the first day, one should consider building a teepee shelter. If not on the first day, then definitely on the second. There are many advantages to a teepee shelter. First, you can build a small fire in a fire pit in the middle of the teepee. Second, the roof is very steep, so rain can run off of it very fast. It is also much more wind-resistant than a lean-to shelter. This shelter can also be made "airtight;" that is, it can be constructed to hold in the heat and smoke of a fire. Some of the same considerations of a lean-to shelter can be made for a teepee shelter. That is, make sure you face your entrance of the teepee away from the expected direction of the strongest winds. Usually, you will want to point your entrance in a Southerly or Southeast direction. If there is a large body of water, point your shelter's entrance in the direction opposite the water. The rainwater will probably come from where the strongest winds will occur.

The teepee shelter should be at least five to six feet tall. It should have a minimum of four framing poles made from tree branches or bamboo (if available) (see figure 2a). The four or five framing poles should cross at the top, with about six inches of the tops of the poles extending from their cross point. Bind these poles at the cross point with your vine material. You should then bind four to five poles horizontally around the width of the teepee with additional vine material (see figure 2b). Look at the "Lean-to Shelter" section of this chapter for what makes good vine material. You are now ready to start adding your leaf material that will make your shelter "waterproof."

The best leaf material will be the broadest leaves you can find. Again, refer to the "Lean-to Shelter" section of the chapter for good leaf candidates. As with the lean-to shelter, you begin placing your leaf material starting from the bottom and make sure to point the leaves downward (see figure 2c). The second layer of leaves needs to overlap the bottom layer of leaves by at least six to eight inches. You should continue placing each additional layer to overlap the previous layer by at least six to eight inches. Continue this process until the entire shelter is covered in leaves. Do not worry that there is a hole at the top of your shelter where the framing poles cross. The rain never falls directly vertically—it always falls at an angle, depending on the direction of the wind. Next, you need to go inside your completed shelter and check the roof for any light shining through. If so, go outside and place additional leaves to cover that potential leak. Lastly, you need to use a few broad leaves to cover the entrance. You should construct your entrance door so that it is easy to place and remove from both inside and outside your shelter. By the way, if you can find some stalks of bamboo, this is the best and most versatile material to use to build your shelter!

JERRY DARSEY

Fig-2a

Fig-2b

Fig-2c

Fig-2d

Fig-2e

Figure 2a–e: Steps for building a teepee shelter

A tremendous advantage of the teepee shelter is that you can build a fire relatively safely inside. The next chapter will cover fire-making, but let's assume you are able to build a fire in the middle of your shelter. You need to dig an eight- to ten-inch-deep pit in the middle of your shelter. Make sure you do not make too big of a fire, however, and keep some water inside your teepee shelter in case embers from the fire land on the inside of your roof. This almost never happens, but you should be prepared just in case. Also, frame your firepit with large rocks (about eight to ten inches in diameter). Now I am from Louisiana, and much of my camping and, in particular, survival camping experiences were in the Louisiana swamps. There are tons of biting insects in the swamps: mosquitoes, sandflies, gnats, etc. Now, if you are in an environment where there are lots of biting insects, you need to gather some "green" material to feed your fire. Green leaves, branches, etc., will be preferable. Also, Spanish moss is a good material to use, if available. This is because green material will produce a lot of smoke. Once the fire begins producing smoke, you should exit your shelter and close off the entrance. From the outside of your shelter, you should begin to see smoke leak out. This is good! Periodically, you need to enter your shelter and rebuild your fire with more green material. Don't let your fire go out. You should continue this process for about one or more hours. What you are doing is saturating the leaves of your shelter with smoke. Insects do not like smoke! When it begins to get dark, you need to change over to dry material for your fire, which produces little smoke. Most places I've camped in get chilly at night. Your fire now needs to assume the role of keeping you warm. A little additional smoke is ok since it will reinforce the smoke previously produced to keep the biting insects out. There is one more advantage to having a fire. If the fire has been burning for a couple of hours, you should have a good supply of ash. Crawling insects hate ash! Snakes hate ash! You should carefully remove as much ash from your fire as possible. Take the ash and distribute it around the perimeter of your shelter. This will discourage crawling insects, snakes, and other pests from entering your shelter. This is because the ash gets into the lungs of these pests and causes them to have difficulty breathing. My experiences on numerous campouts have proven this works. At night, I always made sure I had at least a six- to eight-inch layer of ash around my shelter, and I continually added to it every day.

Finally, after constructing your shelter, you need to place a layer or two of leaves on the ground. The bare ground will remove a lot of body heat, and leaves are a good insulator. Just check the leaves for bugs before you bring them into your shelter. Insects can hide in some of the most interesting places. The more layers of leaves, the warmer you will be.

Before you go to sleep, have an ample supply of wood stored in your shelter so you don't need to hunt for wood in the middle of the night. Just be sure not to put that supply of wood too close to your fire.

To summarize, teepee shelters are superior to other types of shelters. They are best for keeping out rain because of the steepness of the roof. You can safely build a fire within the shelter. They are totally enclosed, in contrast to most lean-to shelters or A-frame (tent-shaped) shelters. They also retain heat very effectively. I have personally been in a teepee shelter where the outside temperature was in the thirties and forties, and the inside of our teepee shelter remained in the sixties and seventies. The only disadvantage I find to a teepee shelter is it takes about an hour longer to construct than other types of shelters.

CHAPTER 2

Building a Fire

When I make plans to go camping, I make sure I have matches. I place my matches in a medicine bottle to keep them dry. As a backup to ensure the matches stay dry, I dip the heads of the matches in wax before putting them in the medicine bottle. I usually bring kitchen "strike anywhere matches" that can be lit using any rough surface. Therefore, the matches are not dependent on having a "striker." These types of matches can be found in most sporting goods stores, Amazon, or eBay. Many people choose to bring a "fire starter," but I find matches much better and easier to use to start a fire. Also, matches are far superior to a fire starter in wet, humid environments.

Now start gathering your wood. Start with very small twigs, about one-eight to one-fourth inch in diameter. Be sure the twigs are very dry. Don't use twigs that are in contact with the ground. Find dry twigs either off the ground or up in the trees. You can check to see how dry a twig is by bending it to see if it snaps. If it bends even slightly without breaking, the wood is not completely dry. If it is truly dry material, it will make excellent fire-starting tinder. You should place the twigs in a teepee arrangement (see figure 3a). Now, after you've made your small teepee with the small twigs, construct another teepee with slightly larger sticks, about one-fourth to one-half inch in diameter, over the smaller teepee (see figure 3b). Leave a small opening at the bottom of the larger teepee in which to stick your match to light the smaller teepee structure (see figure 3c). As your fire grows, you can then add larger and larger pieces of wood to keep it going (see figure 3d). There are other types of structures you can build to make your fire, but this teepee structure is the simplest and most efficient way to get a fire started. It is also good to note that this is the best type of fire to make in the center of your teepee shelter (discussed in chapter 1). However, be careful not to make your fire too big, as you don't want to catch your shelter on fire, and dig a pit in which to build your fire.

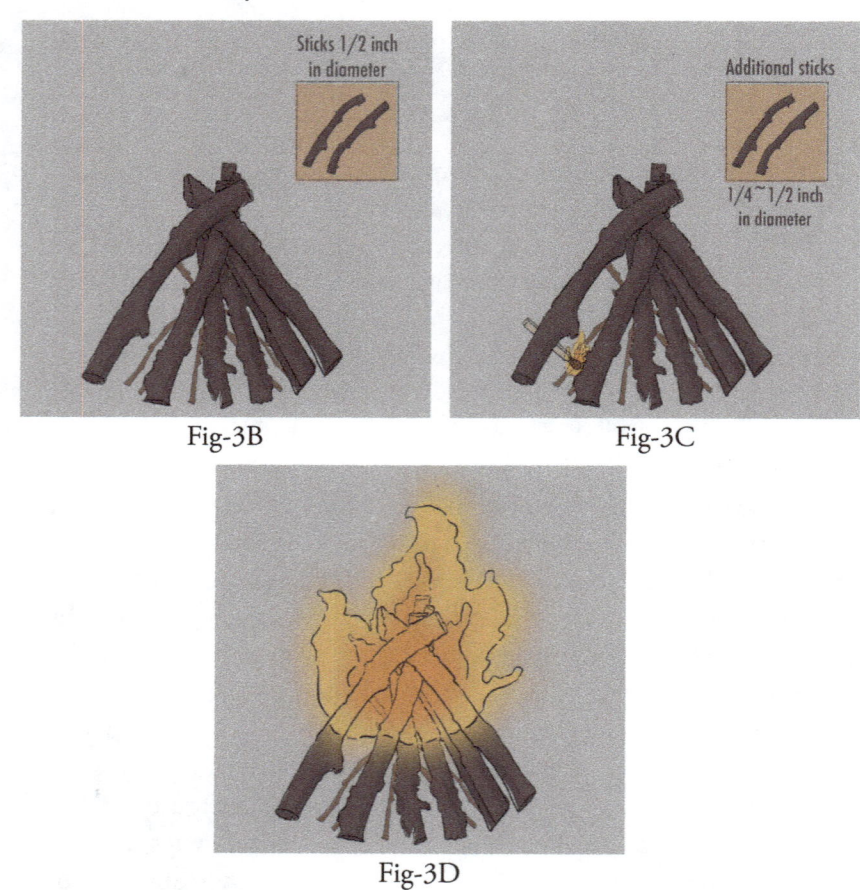

Fig-3B

Fig-3C

Fig-3D

Figure 3b–d: Steps for building a teepee fire structure

After your fire has started and you have built it up to the point that it won't go out, you need to keep adding wood until you have a large pile of ash. You can use this ash to spread around the circumference of your shelter. Crawling insects, small lizards, and snakes do not like to cross the boundary of ash. I was told it gets into their lungs and makes it difficult for them to breathe.

As a side note, I have found that eating plenty of garlic, starting about a week before you go camping, is a good mosquito and biting insect repellant. I don't have scientific proof of this, but it seems to have always worked for me. I've included a reference at the end of this chapter, citing evidence of garlic as a biting insect repellant.

A very important safety consideration is to NEVER leave a fire unattended. Also, before you leave a campsite, thoroughly douse your fire with water. Make sure you stir the coals of the fire to be sure that there are not any hot coals left.

CHAPTER 3

Finding and Purifying Water

Obtaining water, of course, is a very important part of any successful primitive camping trip. When camping in Louisiana, especially in the swamps, there was never a problem with finding water. In fact, the problem that existed there was finding dry land. Of course, not everyone will go camping in the swamps of Louisiana. The problem then becomes where to find a good source of water. If you are in an area where water is not plentiful, look for areas of large, green vegetation. Vegetation is the best indicator of where water can be found. Suppose you are at a place where you can scan the horizon, look for an area where the vegetation seems to be thicker. That will usually indicate where a source of water can be found, and you should head in that direction. If you can't find a hill or place high enough to scan the horizon, climb a tree. You should be able to find at least a small stream of water flowing by the vegetation.

One very important necessity when obtaining any source of water is to make sure the water is potable (safe to drink). The best way to purify water is to boil it. If you have a pot, your first task will be to make a fire (see chapter 2). Make sure you boil the water for at least fifteen minutes. This will ensure that all deadly pathogens have been killed. If you find yourself in a survival situation without a pot, then the issue of boiling becomes more challenging. If you can find a rock formation with a large "dip" in it, you can place water in this indention. In order to boil the water, you can heat up small rocks, no larger than three or four inches in diameter, in the fire you made until the rocks are very hot. The best type of rocks to use are igneous rocks rather than limestone or sedimentary rocks. (See the reference section for a description of different types of rocks.) Now you carefully remove the rocks from the fire, using perhaps sticks to avoid getting burned. Place these very hot rocks in the water that is contained in the dip of the rock formation. After about thirty seconds, remove the rocks from the water and replace them with a new set of hot rocks fresh from the fire. Continue this process for at least fifteen to twenty minutes. After that, your water should be safe enough to drink.

Let's say you're not able to find a suitable rock formation. Don't give up hope! You can look for an area where bamboo is growing. It can almost always be found growing in the swamps. When you come to a large cluster of bamboo, find the largest bamboo stock. These bamboo stocks should be at least six or more inches in diameter. Chop down one or two of these stocks as close to the ground as you can. Haul these stocks back to your camping area. Cut the bamboo on either side of the node (or seam/knot) (see figure 4). The "internode," that is, the space between the nodes, makes an excellent container for your water. You need to cut the top part of the internode area open so the piece of bamboo can hold your water and hot rocks. You then follow the procedure for boiling the water as described in the previous paragraph. If you have difficulty finding a cluster of bamboo, you can try to find a large log and hollow it out to make a container to hold your water. By the way, bamboo also makes excellent building material for any shelter.

Figure 4: Showing using a bamboo stock for holding and boiling water

If you're lucky enough, you may find a formation of rocks where the water is flowing directly out of the rocks. In this case, you can drink the water directly from the flow without concern for purification. Mother Nature has taken care of purifying it for you with natural filtration.

Of course, one of the best sources of potable water is rainwater. If you're in an area where there is plenty of rainwater, that is obviously the best source. The only issue becomes how to collect and store it. The best way to collect rainwater would be to use a large leaf, shape it into a bowl shape and funnel the water into a suitable container. If you do not have a pot, dish, or other suitable container, such as a canteen, you can make a container following the previously mentioned instructions and figure 4 for bamboo or log containers. You can also funnel the water from the roof of your shelter. Rainwater is superior to any other source of water since it's already been purified by Mother Nature.

CHAPTER 4

Obtaining Food

This chapter deals with finding food, both plant and animal. First, If I know ahead of time where I am going to be doing my camping, I will look up the local edible plants in that region. In the swamps of Louisiana, there are many plants that can be eaten. Since the number and variety are very numerous, I will not attempt to describe them in this work. I will provide in the reference section of this book where edible plants can be found.

As for obtaining protein food sources, the easiest animal to find in most environments (and this is particularly true in the swamps of Louisiana) are snakes. It would be wise to research the variety of snakes in the area where you are going camping. Of great importance is to determine if a particular snake is venomous. However, a general "rule of thumb" for a venomous snake is one that has a more triangular head. This is a general rule but certainly not an absolute rule. There are very poisonous snakes that do not necessarily have a triangular head, especially snakes found in water and especially in seawater. My general rule is to assume every snake is poisonous, and therefore, when approaching the snake, proceed with extreme caution. In my experience, the best device to capture a snake is to have a long stick with a forked end (see figure 5). You can sharpen the forked ends of the stick (see fig 5). Your goal is to pin the head of the snake between the two forked ends of your stick. The snake will not be cooperative, so you need to be careful but persistent. As soon as you have pinned the head to the ground, you need to get your knife out (hopefully a large knife) and cut the snake's head off. Be careful! Although you chopped off the head, it is still capable of biting, sometimes for as long as a half hour.

Figure 5: Showing walking stick with a forked end for catching snakes

    Now if you are going to attempt to trap small animals, you need to be observant, especially in areas of about one hundred feet or so around your campsite. Look for trails where small animals frequent. Usually, you can find these trails going to and from a source of water. If you find a probable trail, look for fresh tracks. You need to set your traps along these trails. Also, you need to set multiple traps as well as multiple different kinds of traps. I recommend setting at least six to ten traps. Also, if there is a river, stream, or lake as your source of water, find an area where there is water-covered vegetation. For detailed instructions for different types of traps, see references at the end of chapter 4.

One trap that can be made is a "water trap." When set up in a river, stream, or lake with vegetation, a water trap has a good chance of catching fish. Fish like to hide (especially after it starts to get dark) in the weeds where they feel safe from predators. They also like to eat towards dusk. What you need to do is make an enclosure out of vegetation. The trap has a small entrance, perhaps a foot in diameter. The vegetation is arranged so as to make a large cavity (see figure 6 for illustration). At the back of this cavity, you can place your bait. The best bait to use is small insects, such as crickets, grasshoppers, small beetles, etc. Another good type of water trap to make is a funnel-shaped tube trap made from small, green, flexible branches or bamboo, about a one-fourth inch in diameter. These branches need to be weaved into the shape of a funnel (see figure 7). The fish can enter the large open end of the trap but cannot turn around and ends up getting stuck. You need a good and tempting food source at the closed end of the trap. Large insects, such as the ones mentioned previously, or grubs make good bait. As with your land traps, you need to make several water traps, not just one.

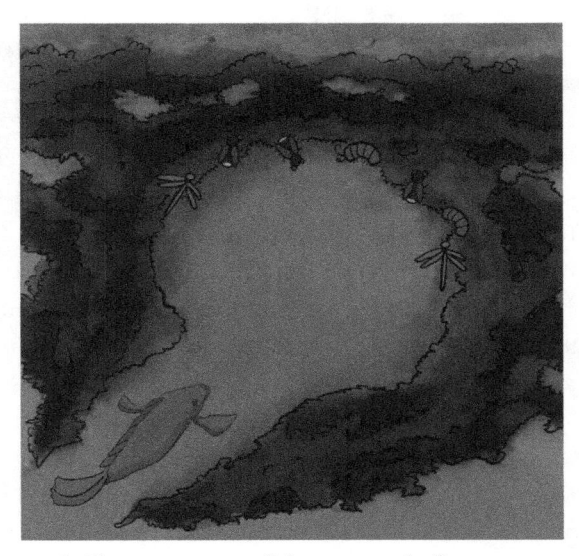

Figure 6: Showing cavity fish trap made from vegetation

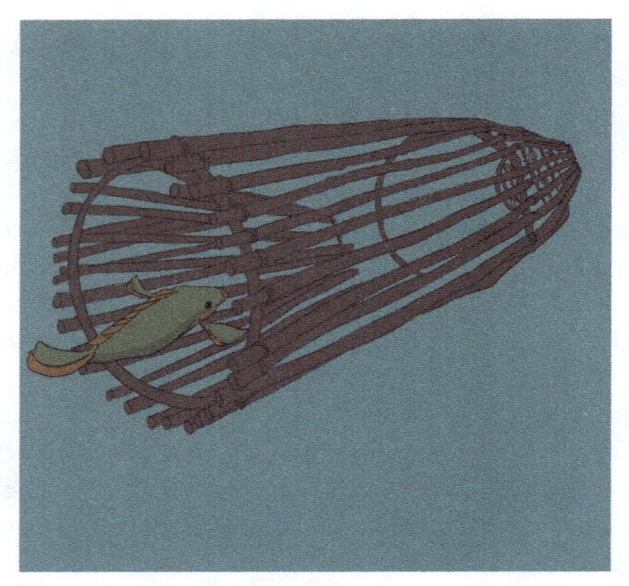

Figure 7: Showing funnel-shape tube trap for catching fish

My most successful trap is one that requires at least somewhat sandy soil. It is sometimes called a "pitfall trap." Most of the time, you can find sandy conditions along the banks of many rivers or shores of lakes and, of course, a beach next to the ocean. What you want to do is dig a hole in the sandy soil, about one to two feet deep. You want the walls of the hole to be about a forty-five-degree angle. The circumference of the top of the hole should be at least one foot, narrowing toward the bottom. You need to place the most rotten piece of meat or flesh of a dead animal you can find at the bottom of the hole. You also need to dig more than one of these types of traps, preferably at least five or six. If you are close to the ocean or a large lake, make sure you dig your hole above the high tide line. The best time to place the bait at the bottom of the traps is at dusk. When you get up in the morning of the next day, almost all of your traps will be filled with small crabs, crawfish, or other small crustaceans. Occasionally, you will also catch small mice and rats. If you catch a small rodent, be very, very careful to cook it thoroughly. Rodents are notorious for carrying parasites. Now, I should point out that most of my camping was in South Louisiana. I feel that most locations, however, where significant amounts of sand are located next to large bodies of water, should have some type of small crustaceans available. The steep walls of the holes you dig will make it impossible for the crabs, crawfish, etc., to crawl out.

If you have a bucket or other container of similar size available, you can use that to trap small animals and crustaceans. Place the bucket where you most likely expect to catch a small game. Place a small piece of wood that is large enough for a small animal or crustacean to crawl up. The top of the piece of wood should be placed against the top of your bucket at no greater than a forty-five-degree angle (see figure 8). Place whatever bait you have at the bottom of the bucket. Your small game with crawl up to the top of the bucket and fall in. The best time to put your bucket out is at twilight. When you check on your bucket the next morning, you should have trapped something. Remember, the best bait for this trap should be the smelliest, most rotten meat you can find.

Figure 8: Showing bucket trap with a ramp for catching small animals/crabs/crawfish

There are a couple of other traps that will help with catching a food source. A trap I particularly like is the "snare trap," which uses a small branch that can be bent down and held in that bent position (see figure 9 for illustration details). You want to place this trap along a path that is obviously traveled by small animals, usually going back and forth from a water source. You want to use very flexible vine material for making the loop that will catch the animal. What may be better than a thin, flexible vine is the roots of the vine. It's been found that the roots are stronger and more flexible than the vine itself. Another point is to strip thoroughly the vine or vine roots to make them as smooth as possible by scraping it with the blade of your knife. Remember, you need it to slip smoothly when an animal trips it. For examples of the best snare traps, see references at the end of this book.

Figure 9: Showing setup of a snare trap

One additional possibility for securing food is to go hunting. If you can find some bamboo, this material makes an excellent spear. Simply shape one end of the bamboo stalk by carving it into a sharp point. To harden the point, you need to fire-polish it—that is, place the spear's point in a fire. However, be careful not to let it catch on fire. Even better would be to stick the point of your bamboo spear in the hot coals of your fire. Leave it in the hot coals for a couple of minutes, again being careful it doesn't catch fire.

CHAPTER 5

Review of Significant Tips

Tips from Chapter 1: Building a Shelter

1. Find a suitable location. Try to locate your shelter close to a water source, avoiding locating it too close. If you have heavy rain, it could overflow the banks of the creek, stream, river, or lake. If you are close to the ocean, or other large bodies of water, be aware of the high tide mark.
2. Point the entrance of your shelter away from the most likely direction of the wind. Usually, the wind comes from the northern or northwest direction. However, if you're close to a large body of water, such as the ocean or a very large lake, the wind will come from the direction of the water.
3. The best type of shelter to build is a "teepee shelter" (see figure 2 in chapter 1). If time is short, the quickest and easiest shelter to build is a lean-to shelter (see figure 1). However, this shelter provides a minimal amount of protection from the elements. A third type of shelter you could build is an A-frame shelter. This shelter provides a little more protection than the lean-to from the elements, but not quite as good as a teepee shelter.
4. One of the advantages of the teepee shelter is that you can build a small fire in the center of it. If you do this, make

A GUIDE TO PRIMITIVE CAMPING

sure you dig a fire pit about 8 to 10 inches deep. Surround the pit with rocks and keep a bucket of water close by in case sparks cause your shelter to ignite. If you keep your fire small enough, this usually is not a problem.

5. If you're camping in a mosquito-infested area (or other biting insects), you want your fire to generate a lot of smoke inside your shelter. This can be done by putting a lot of green or wet material on your fire. Leaves picked off the ground will create a lot of smoke, as will Spanish moss (see bibliography for Spanish moss description).
6. To keep crawling insects and small snakes out of your shelter, take some of the ash from your fire and spread it around the perimeter of your shelter.
7. Don't forget to line your shelter floor with green leaves for insulation.

Tips from Chapter 2: Building a Fire

1. Bring matches. (Not a fire starter!) Make sure you take precautions to keep your matches dry. Dipping the head of the matches in wax, or dripping wax from a candle, will keep them dry. Keeping the matches in a watertight medication bottle will also help to keep them dry.
2. When getting ready to use the matches, remove the wax carefully so as not to damage the head.
3. To construct your fire, begin making a small teepee-shaped structure using the smallest, driest twigs you can find, less than ⅛ to ¼ inch in diameter.
4. Constructed over this small teepee of twigs, is a second teepee of slightly larger sticks, greater ¼ of an inch in diameter. Be sure the material you are using is very dry. Don't use anything touching the ground. The material you use should snap when bent.

5. You should leave a small opening in the second teepee structure to allow yourself the ability to light the smaller, inner teepee with a match.
6. Before lighting your fire, gather and place a sufficient supply of wood close by for keeping the fire going.

Tips from Chapter 3: Finding and Purifying Water

1. The best indication for water is vegetation. In areas where water is plentiful, like in the swamps, vegetation is everywhere. In areas where water is not plentiful, green areas are the best indication of a water source. Go where the green is!
2. Once you find the water, you need to make sure it is suitable to drink. For this, you need to find a way to boil the water. If you have a pot, boiling the water is easy. If you do not have a pot, you need to find something in nature to hold your water. A large divot in a rock formation can be suitable for boiling your water. Heating rocks in your fire can be used to accomplish this. For more details, see chapter 3.
3. Another good way to boil and store your water is a large stock of bamboo. A hollowed-out log could also be used to boil and store the water.
4. You might be lucky enough to find water flowing from a rock formation. This water is already purified by Mother Nature. Another easy way to obtain already purified water is to collect rainwater.

Tips from Chapter 4: Obtaining Food

1. Before going on any planned primitive camping trip, study the edible vegetation for the area where you plan to go camping.
2. Catching and trapping small animals is a potential good source of food. In most environments, the easiest animal

to catch is a snake. You must be very careful however, and assume all snakes are poisonous. Only if you are positive the snake is not poisonous, you can try catching the snake with your hands. Otherwise, use a fork-shaped stick, about 5 feet long, to pin the head of the snake to the ground. Once the head of the snake is secured, get your knife out and chop the head off. Remember, however, that even the severed head can still bite.

3. In finding the best location for a land trap, look for trails made by small animals. These trails are usually found leading to a water source.

4. The easiest way to trap fish is to make a funnel out of branches or bamboo, if it is available. Otherwise, you can make an enclosed cavity out of the vegetation.

5. The easiest trap to make for small animals and/or crustaceans, such as crabs and crawfish, is to dig a hole about two feet deep. The opening of the hole should be at least a foot in diameter and tapering off at least a forty-five-degree angle toward the bottom of the hole. Place your bait in the bottom of the hole. The best type of bait would be the most rotten, putrid-smelling meat you can find. Crabs and crawfish will be especially attracted to this bait.

6. This two-foot hole can also be used to catch small animals, such as mice and rats. However, the best bait for these animals is small insects, such as grasshoppers and crickets.

7. Another type of trap that I recommend is the "snare trap." This trap is particularly useful in catching small animals, such as squirrels and rabbits. The secret to making a good snare trap is to use strong vines or roots of vine material. Scraping the vine material is key to making a good snare trap. See chapter 4 for more details.

8. For catching small animals or fish, I cannot emphasize enough the importance of setting numerous traps and numerous different types of traps! Also, set multiple traps along multiple trails.

ADDITIONAL READING

Chapter 1: Building a Shelter

1. https://pursuingoutdoors.com/how-to-build-a-shelter-in-the-woods/.
2. https://www.prepperssurvive.com/shelter-in-the-woods/.
3. https://www.filson.com/blog/how-to/build-wilderness-survival-shelter/.
4. https://www.fieldandstream.com/story/survival/how-to-build-warm-survival-shelters-in-winter/.
5. https://tipsforsurvivalists.com/beginners-guide-to-building-a-shelter-in-the-woods/.
6. https://theprepperjournal.com/2014/02/18/make-shelter-woods/.
7. https://urbansurvivalsite.com/easy-survival-shelters-beginners/.
8. https://www.survivalworld.com/shelters/types-of-survival-shelters/.
9. https://survivallife.com/build-shelters-using-natural/.
10. https://www.instructables.com/Build-a-Simple-Shelter/.

Chapter 2: Building a Fire

1. https://tinkergarten.com/activities/build-a-fire.
2. https://www.wikihow.com/Build-a-Fire.
3. https://www.rei.com/learn/expert-advice/campfire-basics.html.

4. https://www.popsci.com/how-to-build-a-fire/.
5. https://www.instructables.com/3-Ways-to-Build-a-Fire/.
6. https://www.mossyoak.com/our-obsession/blogs/how-to/camping-hacks-6-different-ways-to-build-a-fire.
7. https://thedyrt.com/magazine/lifestyle/how-to-build-a-campfire/.
8. https://lifehacker.com/how-to-build-a-better-fire-both-outdoors-and-in-5812728.
9. https://www.sunnysports.com/blog/%EF%BF%BChow-to-start-a-fire/.
10. https://www.reserveamerica.com/outdoors/how-to-start-a-campfire.htm.
11. https://homeguides.sfgate.com/garlic-water-ratio-bug-repellent-88909.html.

Chapter 3: Finding and Purifying Water

1. https://geology.com/rocks/igneous-rocks.shtml.
2. https://geology.com/rocks/limestone.shtml.
3. https://education.nationalgeographic.org/resource/sedimentary-rock.
4. https://www.primalsurvivor.net/boil-water-without-pot/.
5. https://www.mensjournal.com/uncategorized/how-to-purify-water-with-hot-rock-boiling#:~:text=The%20answer%20is%20both%20simple,to%20a%20boil%2C%20purifying%20it.
6. https://en.wikipedia.org/wiki/Stone_boiling.
7. https://www.youtube.com/watch?v=jGd6YOE-_8c.
8. https://www.youtube.com/watch?v=JEawdGbv0xg.
9. https://www.youtube.com/watch?v=bIlEjHZgmRg.

Chapter 4: Obtaining Food

1. https://www.wikihow.com/Purge-Crawfish.
2. https://www.youtube.com/watch?v=ewfKVvyeNb4.

3. https://wjbq.com/how-well-did-my-bucket-mouse-trap-work-here-are-the-results/.
4. https://www.youtube.com/watch?v=deT4-NgwbbM.
5. https://www.theavidfisher.com/bucket-crab-trap-tutorial/.
6. https://www.themeateater.com/fish/freshwater/how-to-trap-crayfish.
7. https://www.youtube.com/watch?v=CEmAfWqNsFQ.
8. https://www.pinterest.com/pin/survivordude-how-to-make-a-twitchup-snare--1555149993367954407/.
9. https://www.offgridweb.com/survival/survival-trapping-4-easy-traps-to-learn/.
10. https://ineedthattoprep.com/top-5-easiest-small-animal-traps-to-build-for-beginners/.
11. https://www.thedailygardener.com/how-to-build-a-animal-trap.
12. https://www.wikihow.com/Make-a-Snare-Trap.
13. https://rethinksurvival.com/7-diy-survival-traps-to-know/.
14. https://en.wikipedia.org/wiki/Pitfall_trap.
15. https://www.inaturalist.org/posts/33644-method-7-pitfall-trap.
16. https://survivalskills.guide/best-primitive-survival-fish-traps-how-to/.
17. https://willowhavenoutdoor.com/how-to-make-a-primitive-funnel-fish-trap-that-keep-on-giving/.
18. https://www.americanoutdoor.guide/survival-skills/native-fishing-build-primitive-fish-basket-trap/.

INDEX

A-frame shelter 2, 8, 22
Alligator x
Ashes 7, 8, 11, 23
Bait 17, 18, 19, 25
Bamboo 4, 5, 13, 14, 17, 21, 24, 25
Banana tree leaves 1
Binding material 2, 3
Biting insects ix, 7, 11, 23
Bobcat x
Boil water x, 12, 13, 14, 24
Branches 1, 2, 3, 4, 7, 17, 20, 25
Bucket trap 19, 23
Cordage 2
Coyote x
Crabs 18, 19, 25
Crawfish 18, 19, 25
Crawling insects 7, 11, 23
Crossbar 1, 2, 3
Crustaceans 18, 19, 25
Dry wood 7, 9
Edible plants 15, 24
Fire x, 4, 7, 8, 9, 10, 11, 12, 13, 21, 22
Firepit 4, 7
Fire-polish 21
Fire starter 9, 23
Fish trap 17
Floor covering 4
Framing poles 4, 5
Garlic 11
Gnats 7

Green material 7, 23
Hight-tide 2, 18, 22
Hot coals 11, 21
Hot rocks 13
Insect repellant 11
Leaf material 1, 4, 5
Lean-to shelter 1, 2, 3, 4, 5, 8, 22
Locating water 19
Matches 9, 10, 23, 24
Medicine bottle 9
Mice 18, 25
Mosquitoes 7, 11, 23
Palmetto leaves 1
Palm tree leaves 1
Pine needles 4
Pitfall trap 18
Potable 12, 14
Purifying water x, 12, 14, 24
Rain ix, x, 1, 2, 4, 5, 8, 22
Rainwater 4, 14, 24
Rats 18, 25
Rock formation 13, 24
Roofing material 4, 5, 7
Sand flies 7
Shelter x, 1, 2, 4, 5, 7, 8, 10, 11, 13, 14, 22, 23
Smoke 4, 7, 23
Snake x, 7, 11, 15, 16, 23, 25
Snare trap 20, 25
Spanish moss 7, 23
Spear 21

Sticks x, 9, 13, 23
Strike anywhere matches 9
Swamps ix, x, 7, 12, 13, 15, 24
Teepee fire 10
Teepee shelter 4, 6, 7, 8, 10, 22
Tracks 16
Twigs 9, 23
Vegetation 12, 16, 17, 24, 25
Venomous snakes 15
Vine roots 20

Vines 2, 3, 4, 20, 25
Walking stick x, 16
Water source 2, 20, 22, 24, 25
Water trap 17
Wax 9, 23
Wet wood 9, 23
Wind direction 2, 22
Wolves x

ABOUT THE AUTHOR

Jerry Darsey is a professor in the Department of Chemistry and director of the Center for Molecular Design and Development (cmdd.ualr.edu) at the University of Arkansas at Little Rock. His BS degree is in physics, and his PhD is in chemistry, both from Louisiana State University. Dr. Darsey is the author or co-author of approximately two hundred manuscripts in numerous referred journals. However, this book is based on the author's experiences in the Boy Scouts of America while growing up in Houma, Louisiana. The author was in the Boy Scouts from the age of eleven to eighteen. He was also a counselor for four years at the New Orleans area council Boy Scout camp in Slidell, Louisiana. When Jerry became a father, his son joined the Boy Scouts at age eleven, and Jerry became the assistant Scoutmaster for Troop 12 in Little Rock, Arkansas. During all these years involved in the Boy Scouts, he has gone on hundreds of camping trips, including many survival camping trips. The inspiration for writing this book was due to the numerous "survival" TV reality shows, in which many of the participants seem to not know very much about survival, which this author learned very early in the Boy Scouts. The author, therefore, decided to share his knowledge and experiences with the general public in hopes that it will help the avid primitive camper to the casual weekend-camper.